Acts of Liberation

Opening the Box to Self-Transformation

Ebony I. Green

Praise for *Acts of Liberation*

Acts of Liberation is a catalyst towards a journey of self-reflection and metamorphosis. Dr. Green's vulnerable and honest look at the foundations on which we build our sense of self empowers the reader to push boundaries and explore negative or unhealthy thought patterns. Guided questions and statements of purpose help unlock deeply held beliefs that shape how we communicate, relate and react; leaving the reader open to challenge the way they view their place in the world. Dr. Green's writing speaks a universal truth: in unwrapping, accepting and celebrating the greatness of our perfectly imperfect humanity, we rise.

- Carrie Frost

This book is medicine for the soul! It revealed the suppressed tower moments in my own life and reinforced the need to "sit in it" and process my feelings instead of rushing to solutions. I'm genuinely grateful for the vulnerability shown by Dr. Green and her willingness to unpack her journey so that we can all begin to heal. What a fantastic and timely read as our world cries for more humanity and less pain.

- Dynell Kellyman

The honesty shared in *Acts of Liberation* make the idea of breaking free not only seem possible, but joyful! Ebony Green patiently and carefully walks the reader through those "Tower Moments" that changed her life and opened the opportunity for her healing. As she experiences healing, she invites us it our own. This book liberates and encourages each of us to discover our "soul purpose."

- Yolanda Sealey-Ruiz

Praise for *Acts of Liberation*

This book serves almost as a guide to the process of healing one's self from past traumatic or life-altering events in a way that allows readers to conform the morals of the book to one's personal situation. It does not matter what you are at in your life journey. Whether readers think they have everything figured out or are just starting their process of self-discovery and self-actualization, the author has a way of inserting joy and comfort into her words that make it enjoyable and insightful for anyone.

- Eric Irkliewskij

As a social worker, I see this book as having great potential for helping people identify patterns and themes as they examine the deeper meaning and connections in tower moments. Dr. Green explains how this helps us to not only evolve towards the best version of ourselves but also helps us to understand our true purpose. I found reading this book is a valuable investment in self. It is the type of book that one can read and re-read, finding deeper meaning each time...*Acts of Liberation* will not only help the reader make sense of challenging moments in their lives, but as Dr. Green explains, this understanding helps us to realize our own unique gifts and in doing so, we can then make meaningful impact in the world.

- Amy Pittari

"Acts" proved to be a dynamic guide to leading me on an authentic journey of self-reflection and actualization. I highly recommend this book to be used as a roadmap for those who aspire to be and are leaders to increase their effectiveness as they strive for alignment in their personal and professional lives.

- Sybil Knight-Burney

Acts of Liberation

Opening the Box to Self-Transformation

Ebony I. Green

Kaleidoscope Vibrations LLC
New York, New York
2022

Requests for permission to make copies of any part of this book should be emailed to:
publishing.kvibrations@gmail.com

Printed in the United States of America.

ISBN 978-1-949949-05-6

Cover artwork and illustrations by Logic Thompson.
Cover design & book design by Caroline Rinaldy.

First printing, 2022

www.kvibrations.com

This book is dedicated to Mom and Dad, Evonne and Harold Green Jr. Thank you for bringing me into this world. Thanks, mom, for always being there, to laugh, to cry, to love me. Your support has allowed me to continue to grow into my best self. Dad, even though you passed away when I was young, you have forever shaped my journey. Thank you both because without you there would be no me. I love you! This book would not have been possible without the gifts of your presence in my life creating the path and establishing a legacy of intelligence, hard work, persistence, and resilience.

Contents

Introduction

There are times that challenge everything we believe about the world and even what we believe about ourselves. I refer to these moments as tower moments. In some spiritual communities, the tower can symbolize sudden upheaval, loss, and unexpected change. The tower can also create space for something new.

Tower moments are unplanned, life changing experiences. We have all experienced many tower moments — struggling through some of them, conquering some of them, and even finding our faith in hardship. But we rarely gain a true understanding of the role these moments play in our spiritual and emotional growth. We struggle to contextualize these experiences because we attempt to view them through our heads or our hearts. We use our intellect, trying to understand why we are thrust into these moments, or we react by succumbing to our emotions. We need to merge the head and the heart to fully understand how tower moments support alignment with our true purpose. This perspective enables us to make sense of tower moments as opportunities offering insight.

The intention of this book is threefold: to explain what tower moments are; to help you understand how to make meaning of these moments in your life; and to clarify how these experiences help to unlock evolutionary change.

This process is not finite but cyclical; harnessed properly, it will help you find your "soul purpose." You will learn to use tower moments to ground yourself in the growth process. By recognizing your worth and what gifts you bring to transform the world, you can stand firmly in who you are. This work can help you to liberate your mind, body, and soul to access true freedom. True freedom in many cases is the freedom to live your life without limiting beliefs about yourself.

Life is not happening to us, rather, we are actively partaking in it. In coming to a heightened awareness of our spiritual selves, we gain awareness that our outside circumstances are, in part, manifestations of our thoughts, beliefs, and actions. If we look at life in a positive way, much of life works to align in positive patterns. When we choose the lens of negativity, life reflects those negative beliefs and thoughts back to us. Awakening uncovers the connection between our thoughts and our outcomes, and we become empowered to make choices that guide us towards our "soul purpose."

We can choose to do the work willingly or, during a tower moment, be forced to do the work. This struggle is part of the human experience. You are not alone.

Introduction

Chapter 1
The Tower: Building on a Flawed Foundation

Life happens, often leaving us to wonder what went wrong. Solving that mystery starts with two questions: What went right? And when did it start to feel wrong?

Tower moments can be small events or experiences that result in confusion or uncertainty, or they can be more significant and lead to sudden upheaval. They are recognizable when a situation in your life causes chaos, makes you feel unsteady, and uncomfortable. It is when you lose control of the situation; when you experience clear signs that something is amiss but continue to press on. As disruptive as they seem, these moments are in our life to provide opportunities to grow, explore, and move toward our best self. **Tower moment are opportunities to identify themes or issues within your life that should be explored.**

In my experience, when red flags appeared, I should have paused and taken inventory of my life. But I didn't! Red flags can often be explained as interactions or situations that you intuitively know are not good for you. Instead of removing yourself, you tend to say, "it's not really that bad" or minimize the potential harm people, places, or things can bring to our life. I didn't think I had the strength or energy for such reflection. I wanted to ignore the moments and simply continue with my life.

When I failed to heed the warnings, I experienced tower moments. Tower moments are unmistakable because when you are in that dark, you cannot see any way out. But to continue as a whole and complete human, the work needs to be done. I instinctively clenched tightly, desperate to control the outcome. In those moments, holding on too tightly only makes things worse. My life turned upside down and the upheaval was exhausting. In such moments, what is occurring externally is a manifestation of what is undone internally. The pain we experience reflects the chaos that lives within us. For me, most often, it was pain or trauma that I masked until it could no longer be ignored.

My first tower moment happened when I was a young girl, I can still remember the moment my mom got the news. We were sleeping in my mother's bed with her because my brother and I were afraid to sleep alone. My dad had battled cancer for what felt like an eternity but was, in reality, approximately 1 year. I was only seven when he passed; it was a large part of my young life. I vividly remember the day he died. It was Mother's Day morning at 1:35 am when the phone rang. My mom answered the phone. It was someone from the hospital calling to notify her that my dad had died. I acted like I was asleep but intuitively knew what the call meant. Even now I'm not sure how I knew but I knew. I remember the moment the phone rang; I woke up and heard my mother answer the phone in a monotone way. I could hear the sadness in her voice while she had the brief exchange over the phone.

As she hung up the phone, I felt numb and disconnected from my self. The feeling of listening as my mother received that news will always be with me. It felt as if something broke inside me. Like a light was turned off. In that moment I felt, angry, sad, hurt and a part of me blamed him for leaving us. How does a child that age ever process death? Over the course of time, that confusion turned from relief to sadness to fear. Though I did not realize it at the time, this experience was the foundational tower moment of my life. In that moment, I interpreted the situation in multiple ways that were neither good nor true. I developed an illogical yet deep sense of abandonment. The feeling of abandonment haunted and still haunts me. But now, I see it, observe it, and let it go. As an adult, I wonder how the rest of my family unit experienced this tower moment. Could we all be sharing the same tower, if so, what is the story we told ourselves?

Before I started my path to healing, I was at a loss; I had never felt truly whole and complete. It was impossible to identify what I was missing out on because I didn't know what whole or complete looked or felt like. I could not relate to feeling whole and complete until the healing began to take place. I could only touch the surface of feeling emotionally well balanced, but I needed to go below the surface.

Tower moments signify a flawed foundation. Anything built on a flawed foundation will crumble in time because these foundations were never built to weather storms. By tearing down what is not solid, by uncovering that which we have buried below the surface, tower moments provide a transformational opportunity to rebuild a more solid foundation. But if we try to move on without first sifting through the rubble, we will rebuild on the same flawed foundation, continuing on the same path that results in more cycles of the same tower moments.

Take heart: these experiences are part of our growth journey. Life is an iterative process, and these moments are just another iteration of trying to reach your whole and complete self.

Another profound tower moment occurred when I abruptly lost a close relationship. We were good and then we were not. All I was left with were questions: Why didn't I see this coming? What did or didn't I do to contribute to this end? Why didn't I work harder at fixing it? I had no real explanation or clarity. All I could come up with was that I was not good enough, not worthy of another chance. I questioned if the sacrifices were worth it and if we ever loved each other. The answers I gave myself in that moment were nowhere near the truth and did not get at the heart of the matter. I could not recognize that such responses were symptoms of a broader internal problem.

1

The Tower: Building on a Flawed Foundation

When my relationship ended, I cried from my soul. I cried all the tears I had swallowed for so long; the tears seemed endless, and I was unable to stop them. I thought I was going to lose my mind. I was merely existing within my pain. I needed to step out of the pain to realize what I was missing. Tower moments exist because God, the universe, the great spirit, whatever you choose to call it, creates space for us to feel whole and complete. But becoming whole sometimes requires tearing down what was initially built. I could not reach my true purpose until I dealt with my emotional baggage. Like most people, I had spent my entire life trying to hide from myself. This had not served me well.

The end of my relationship shook me to my core. In retrospect, all the emotion attached to the experience was a purging. I purged all the lies that had come to live within me. Crying cleansed me and helped me let go. I shed what no longer served me. I wept, I slept, and I sat in silence, seeking meaning in everything I was unable to reconcile. I can only describe it as a constant state of irritation. I guess it was really desperation. This was the moment! The moment when you are so tired of ending up in the same place that something must change. I just knew I was tired and needed to do something different. I used to sit and marvel at other people who appeared so happy, so joyous, so confident of where they were going. I wanted that. I wanted to find the place that others had reached, and I had no idea how to do it. These questions were the start of my self-exploration as I sought to alleviate the discomfort I felt. I asked, "What must I get rid of?"

"How do I let go of what no longer serves me?" "What does it even mean to let go of what no longer serves me?" I needed to know what was no longer good for me – mentally, physically, or spiritually, and what I needed to change to experience a better outcome.

In the process of asking these questions, it appeared that I had never experienced a loss that felt this intense before. I knew this experience was not simply about losing my current relationship. The pain was older and deeper than the present. I awakened to a common theme I had ignored until now. I saw that something needed to change and felt the something that needed to change was me.

As I sought answers, I investigated the layers of my tower and came to recognize that I was growing and evolving in a way that I could not explain. While other moments in life had been extremely difficult, this time felt radically different. It felt like this moment was aligned to my life path. I can't explain why or how I knew that this moment related to my life path, but I did. I'm unsure if the moment really was different or if I had matured.

At some point I began to realize that my tears were from far more trauma than the loss of any single relationship. In fact, they were from the loss of many relationships that I had failed to grieve. In my case, the tears stemmed from the initial loss of my father when I was 7 years old, and my inability to process that loss. When my father died, I developed a feeling of unworthiness. My 7-year-old self-concluded that he died because I was not worthy of love or because he did not love me. I told myself that if we were worth it, he would have fought harder. Both conclusions were wrong, as is bound to happen when a 7-year-old is the one drawing them. I loved my father immensely and losing him was traumatic. I believed that I would never love anyone else that much. I believed that every time I loved someone with all of me, they would die or leave. I believed that I wasn't worthy. That I didn't deserve love. My false conclusion birthed a lie that would haunt every relationship from that moment onward.

Over the years the lie was reinforced through a series of events that served as "evidence" demonstrating that, despite my successes, I was still unworthy, that there was something wrong with me. As I grew older, I inadvertently sought out people who reaffirmed the lies that I believed about myself. I didn't know that those around me were reinforcing the lie. I didn't even know that what I believed was not the truth. The lies we tell ourselves sabotage our growth and perspective. If we don't investigate these lies, they will continue to hijack our progress. I could not recognize that there was a root cause to my spiral. My unresolved scarring left me vulnerable to these external forces; these interactions reinforced that the lie was true. The lie grew in me like a parasite. My first tower moment, when I was seven, created a faulty foundation that future moments of similar loss were built upon.

Each of us lives with our own lies — their weight is carried forward from childhood. For me, this burden shaped the way I engaged with the world. The lie led me to put myself in situations that didn't serve me well. I mimicked the unloving behaviors of others and began to treat myself in unloving ways. I minimized myself and, as a result, believed that the way I was treated and the situations I was in were all I deserved. In thinking less of myself, I falsely reassured myself that I was not entitled to more. In this mindset, my "best life" left me less than whole and complete; it was time to question whether I was in the right place. I started to explore these questions because I realized my answers were built on a flawed foundation. I needed to go deeper, to dig down below the answers I had relied on.

The abrupt end of my relationship with my partner was an opportunity for the lie I'd told myself to meet the truth. Only two paths were illuminated. I could step on the path of self-denial, or I could start to really examine the loss. My inclination was self-denial. The work just seemed too hard. I resorted to my lie: I was not, nor would I ever be worthy of love. I did not recognize the theme of worth for what it was, yet it had been playing out in all facets of my life. I had negatively internalized this sense that I was not worthy, and so it continued to grow.

The lie is complex and must be carefully deconstructed. Once I simplified the lie in my head, I trivialized its existence. I believed I could live with it. Finally, I was forced to consider the quality of my life in that context. I could live, but could I live well? I had to define what I needed, but for a long time the lie prevented me from doing so which limited my happiness. With that lie, I could never aspire to the great heights intended for me.

The Tower: Building on a Flawed Foundation

Unearthing the lie about my worth was essential to moving forward on my journey. I had to work backwards and figure out where I had lost my way. I had to uncover the story that I told myself when I lost my dad as a child. Understanding where I first lost myself helped me heal my heart. I became aware that my dad's death, my first tower moment, led me to lose sight of who I could be and that I was deserving of love. To heal, I had to reconcile that my dad dying did not mean that he did not love me.

The lie I had carried deep within my foundation did not serve my wellbeing. This false foundation was preventing me from fulfilling my life purpose. Since the original foundations were not properly established, real inner work had to be undertaken before I could rebuild. I needed awareness and a deep understanding of what was not established correctly to fix it.

When false foundations crumble, it allows us to rebuild on higher ground.

Remember, **tower moments** can be small events or experiences that result in confusion or uncertainty, or they can be more significant and lead to sudden upheaval. They are recognizable when a situation in your life causes chaos, makes you feel unsteady, and uncomfortable.

Guiding questions:

1. What tower moments have you had that you were unable to understand?

2. What happened to cause these moments? What was the root of your pain?

3. What are the patterns that you have had to reconcile before?

4. What have these moments forced you to observe and explore?

These questions are a great start — as they lead you to other doors, open them, and explore further.

1

The Tower: Building on a Flawed Foundation

Chapter 2
Throat Chakra: The Gateway Outside Yourself

As I struggled with the loss of my relationship, I was surprised to discover my inability to communicate effectively, to express myself. Some refer to the inability to communicate effectively as a "closed throat chakra." The throat chakra is in the center of your throat and is linked to knowing and communicating your inner truth. It's the gateway that takes what is inside of you and manifests it outwardly, through words. When your throat chakra is open, you can communicate clearly. A closed throat chakra blocks you from communicating your thoughts, wants, and needs.

Typically, talking comes naturally to me but I didn't have the words because I did not have clarity. I was extremely frustrated. My heart hurt and I was in pain, but I couldn't explain why, where it came from, or how to make it stop. I was impatient when people asked me "what was wrong" or "what happened" because I felt like I had no answers. In my mind I kept saying "Why are you asking me so many questions. If I had the answers, I would give them to you or better yet, I wouldn't be in this situation."

When I tried to explain the discontent I felt, it came out distorted and unclear. I wondered what was wrong with me. NOTHING was wrong with me. But I needed time to process my thoughts and feelings, to make meaning of the experience. In retrospect, I can chuckle at my own garbled attempts to communicate because they were a sign that helped me realize I was in a tower moment.

This was my moment to take a "time out." I was unable to communicate because I needed to reflect before I spoke. I needed to "just sit in it." While communication was key, rushing my process was futile. I made multiple attempts to say what I was feeling only to realize that I did not know what I was feeling. The goal is to respond, not react. When we react, we tend to be impulsive and defensive. We are not able to look at the situation objectively. When we respond, we have taken the time to process the situation and are then able to express ourselves in a balanced and clear manner. To get there, I needed to slow down and have an inner dialogue about what I was feeling. I needed to reconnect with the emotions that I had disconnected from so many years ago, when I had lost my dad. I asked myself, "What are you trying to say and why can't you understand what you're thinking?" When I finally stopped reacting to the upheaval that I was left with in this tower moment, I realized I needed to be quiet and reflect on what it was that I was feeling.

Intuitively, I knew it was time to be silent and figure out what came next. But I also felt compelled to project that all was well to the outside world. Knowing when to speak and when to stay silent was a central theme during this process. At first it was frustrating. I needed space to heal and be introspective about what I needed to do to reach a state of calm. I was trying to figure out how to make the space to work on myself and how to balance that with being the person I always was to everyone else.

I wondered how I could ask others for space without signaling that I was in trouble. I had never created boundaries or learned how to ask for my own space. Each time I tried to explain how I was feeling, I sounded incoherent. My attempts at communication only made the situation worse. Knowing what I wanted to say was important, but I also needed to be able to express myself with compassion. In these tower moments, anger drowned out my reasoning. As long as I was kept blaming everyone else for my being at this point, rational communication was impossible.

Friends asked me what was wrong. In this period of reflection, instead of feeling compelled to supply them with an answer, I let them know I needed some time to figure out how I felt. My silence was new and it made people around me uncomfortable. Some wanted to "fix it" and others pulled away because they personalized my need to be silent, interpreting it as me being cold or uncaring to them. Both reactions made me feel worse. I was used to ignoring my needs to attend to others and this time I could not. For the first time in my life, I didn't need to speak. I could take advantage of not having the answer. I became introverted and didn't want to engage or have conversations. I spent my time by myself, with myself, reflecting on how I felt.

I started to question why I struggled to voice my wants and needs. I uncovered another internalized lie: I believed that even if I communicated my wants and needs, they would remain unmet because my voice was not powerful enough. I started to recognize the connection between how I communicated and my feelings of worth. I began to see how this lie had permeated all aspects of my life.

As I slowed down, I observed how this lie left me surrounded by some individuals who only appeared to have the same values and beliefs as me. I fell prey to people who cared superficially. In this tower moment, I felt pushed to evaluate every relationship in my life. This was an opportunity to evaluate the patterns or themes that exist within our relationships that might be undermining who we truly are, the magic that we possess, and the power that we can bring to the world.

When engaging in an awakening, we discover the parts of life, and parts of ourselves, that must be redefined. Until we make peace with that need to redefine what we once considered core assumptions, we struggle. Instead of recognizing that communicating my needs was a path to freedom, I questioned and judged myself. How would my statement be received? Would I be thought of differently because I had needs? Would I be rejected? I knew what I wanted and what I needed but I didn't know how to say it without worrying that it would not be heard. And so, I didn't say it.

I judged myself because I didn't have the courage to say what I needed. In reflecting on where this behavior came from, I realized that the only one I could blame was myself. I was the reason I was in this moment.

In retrospect, I understand the tower moment had been drawing near for a long time. For years there were red flags, yet I chose to ignore them. At the time, I had no clue what to do. Alone and lost, I felt that sharing my confusion or my pain with others would only serve as fodder for them to gossip about me. Now I recognize that we all have these moments. They may look and feel unique but, in reality, they are ubiquitous.

For so long, I focused on what other people thought about my decisions. I finally understood that making changes for other people to love and value me wasn't serving me. I leaned into what would make them happy instead of what made me happy.

As long as I continued to look outside myself for validation, I permitted others' perceptions and misconceptions to squash my dreams, hopes, and aspirations. It felt as if the people who were supposed to have my back did not; as if I was not living up to their expectations of me; as if their needs and wants superseded my own. But waking up meant that I was not a victim and that it was up to me to prevent this from happening.

I had to examine the relationships in my life and determine which ones reinforced or benefited from my lie. I needed to learn to set appropriate boundaries and stick to them without resentment. I would no longer sacrifice my happiness to serve what I thought others needed from me. Establishing those boundaries and communicating my needs was essential to finding freedom.

In retrospect, there were those who did see my light and nurtured and encouraged my ability to impact the world in positive ways and there were those who were unable to do so. As I began to uncover my false narrative, I realized these people were intertwined and connected to it. These were people I thought I had great relationships with at one point or another. As I began to grow and see the world through a different lens, I wanted them to change and grow right along with me. Healthy relationships require individuals to pour into each other. When you reach a place that you or they are unable to be reciprocal in that process, it is time to part ways. My freedom came at the expense of leaving behind some people that I loved deeply. I realized that many of these people were living out their own lie and that they were a mirror to me. In their broken-ness, I saw my own. I was neither better nor worse than them.

While the work happens within, the changes we make or don't make still impact other human beings. My decisions and actions had repercussions and while

I survived the repetition of my tower moments, I had to become aware of the carnage I left behind. I had to become mindful of my actions as I began this journey. I never went wrong when making decisions with integrity but when I moved away from my true purpose, I did not always make right and just decisions. The further I strayed from my "soul purpose," the more imminent the tower moment was.

People are placed on our paths for different reasons. The challenge was in distinguishing who was there to do what. For me, some provoked me to understand my true power; others assisted me in harnessing it. Some provoked me in ways for which I was unprepared or ways I could not discern. Some showed up as caring individuals but tended only to themselves. With many, I believe their impact was unintentional. At that point they and I were equally unaware of the enormity of what we were on earth to create or discover. Without that perspective, we were all stuck.

Once I understood that this tower moment was in my life to teach me something, I was better able to communicate about it and to make meaning of its' purpose in my life. One important lesson I had to learn was how to effectively communicate my needs and wants to people I cared about. Though I thought I communicated well, I came to realize I only communicated what wouldn't impact me emotionally. I could talk endlessly about any topic other than myself. Yet when someone asked me direct questions, I often responded with "I don't care," "whatever you want," or "I need time to think about it." I would respond indecisively though I knew what I wanted to say.

My inability to communicate effectively kept me in a cycle that negatively impacted my circumstances and made it difficult for me to escape them — over and over again. The same themes were running through my everyday life, repeating across different relationships. Professionally, I worked diligently to impact children in the schools that I led while simultaneously looking for recognition to validate that I was smart enough. In intimate relationships and with friends — irrespective of who I was engaging with — I looked for affirmation that I was enough.

When I didn't feel that others recognized my ability, I internalized that I was not enough. But validation is an inside job. Tower moments repeat if we cannot see the cycle. We must know our worth independently. Otherwise, we move through the world making meaning of how others interact with us - allowing them to confirm or deny our value.

The most important part of the process was to be honest with myself and do all that I could to lift up my truth. "My truth," not "the truth." Everyone has their own lie and their own truth. This is the value of going through this process alone. It was not that I could not ask for help and support, but I needed to ensure that I was observing my own thoughts and not being distracted or swayed by someone else's belief or vision.

I began to spend more time thinking about what brought me joy and what I was passionate about instead of how my choice looked to others. This shift in mindset positioned me to work in a place that brought me joy. With it came a feeling of freedom and fulfillment. In my heart, I knew I was in the right place at the right time on my journey.

I changed jobs because I felt silenced. My new job gave me an opportunity to speak to thousands of people. Often, after my talks, people would approach me to share how my words affected them. I realized this impact was not driven by the topic I discussed but rather the way that I made them think, feel, and dream of possibility. I reminded my audience of the things that I needed to hear: how they were perfectly imperfect and that their broken pieces were worthy of love. The more I was able to be my most authentic self, the more I was able to help them see themselves in context.

I saw that my throat chakra had been blocked long before I realized it was. Identifying this blockage and taking time to figure out how to communicate my wants and needs was a critical part of my journey. When the time came, the universe created space for me to express myself. I knew I was ready when I was able to express how I felt in a balanced way.

My ability to communicate was profoundly felt by those around me. I was able to help them make sense of and gain deeper understandings about complex situations. By sharing my learnings with them, I was helping to raise the collective consciousness of the universe. This was the beginning of understanding my soul purpose.

Guiding Questions:

1. When do you struggle to communicate your emotions effectively?

2. What happens when you try to explain what you are feeling or experiencing before you truly understand what you are feeling or experiencing?

3. How and when do you reshape your feelings, wants, or needs based on others' opinions?

4. How are your feelings, wants, or needs received?

5. How and when do you express your thoughts and feelings clearly, unapologetically, & compassionately?

2

Throat Chakra: The Gateway Outside Yourself

Chapter 3
The Shuffle: Who's to Blame?

In tower moments my instinct was to blame those who had hurt me, but the harsh truth was that I shared the blame. My lie could only be reinforced because I was willing to stay stuck and blind to the truth. I was shown the truth many times before I was ready to accept it and to do the soul work.

Throughout my life, in numerous relationships and interactions with others, there were many times when I walked away or shut a door because I believed the other person was at fault. Some examples of this are feeling left out of a social situation even though I was invited but chose not to go; questioning love or intention when I was not fully showing up or giving love freely; having expectations of others, yet already knowing who they were;

spending more time focused on being right than on coming to a constructive resolution.

To move forward in the healing process, it was essential for me to acknowledge that I had created the situations that resulted in my feeling of emptiness. In the last chapter, I shared my inability to voice my wants and needs, often acquiescing to what others wanted. No one was supposed to make decisions for me but ME. Failing to express my needs took me out of the decision-making role. I had manifested this outcome through inaction.

Accepting responsibility for the circumstances I found myself in was difficult. When tower moments occurred, I looked at the people around me as suspects, believing they ruined my life. I would often be aggravated with those around me, sometimes even shutting people out of my life. The reality is that they did not cause my tower moments, and so, unsurprisingly, removing them from my life did not eliminate the struggles I experienced.

When I was trapped in the blame game, I lived in a world of distraction, avoiding the real work. I perseverated on who was at fault instead of focusing on the root cause of the situation. It was an alluring distraction because blaming someone else took some of the weight off my shoulders – though only temporarily. It is a natural desire to absolve ourselves of responsibility. Absolution is easier than owning the reality of manifesting a self-sabotaging outcome. Eventually I realized I was fooling myself and only making it worse. Blame was irrelevant. Instead of assigning responsibility to someone else, I embraced the obligations I had to myself. It was easier to look outward but, in the end, I was responsible for looking inwards and at the decisions I made. It was hard to admit that I had not been wronged, that I had been a bystander in a life I was meant to lead. During this time, I asked myself:

What was I taught about healing and whose responsibility is it to heal me? What self-work is necessary for healing, who guides that work and how?

These questions took me far along my journey to self-discovery. Each led me to ask and answer more questions about myself. If you are reading this book, you have already realized that true self-discovery must begin with asking the tough questions we often avoid. When I realized that, I needed to determine if I could summon the courage to keep asking the difficult questions and honestly reflecting on the answers.

Once I arrived at this place, I saw there were only two ways I could emerge: bitter or better. While uncomfortable, this was my moment to grow. If I was unwilling to look at and process my past experiences, I would become bitter. If I did reconcile and forgive them, then I could move forward to a better life. One without resentment. The outcome was up to me.

Blame served no purpose in dealing with what was undone in my life. I shifted from blaming people to understanding the role they played in triggering me to do my own life work. The people I blamed were the catalysts I needed for success. Each taught me something that assisted me to become a better human being. As I began to do the work of true healing, I recognized my own role in forcing myself towards a place of expansion. As I began to do my own internal work, I began uncovering the answer to why we make self-harming decisions.

I was my own worst critic. Unable to have compassion for the missteps I had made, I fell into cycles of self-blame. The blame morphed into self-hatred and self-destructive behaviors. This pattern is counterproductive: by focusing on the who, I overlooked the what, how, and why. In this process, I had to be careful of judging myself so harshly that I blocked my own healing. It was painful to realize I had not been kind or just to myself. We can become invested in viewing ourselves in a negative way. I told myself I was stupid. I was not stupid. At times naïve or blind to the truth but not stupid. Self-compassion is the only way to move through this stage. I am a spirit having a human experience. Within that reality, feeling real emotions including pain, guilt, sorrow, and loss is right and necessary. This was an epiphany. It helped me move from blame to examination and to look beneath my surface experiences at the core issue, which was rooted in worth and value.

Allow yourself to experience these emotions but do not sit in blame or guilt for too long. Instead, I invite you to try to examine these emotions as an observer. Try to identify what emotions you are feeling, allow yourself to feel them, and then move on.

Emotions are like guests – some pleasant, some tolerated but all welcome for their time. Explore your response to each of them and then, when it's time for them to move on, let them go. Letting go does not happen overnight. Some situations are easier than others. When I explored a situation that was difficult, I would take the time necessary to process my feelings toward it. There are situations that I continue to process today.

As I sat with my emotions, I began to realize this feeling of loss was all too familiar. This is the place I often ended up. For the first time, I realized that I had all the material things I wanted but no peace of mind. I saw that this deep dissatisfaction and sadness were familiar and cyclical in my life. This time felt worse than ever. Fortunately, I had matured and could see the part I played in getting where I was and how I felt. I saw that looking outside myself would not make me feel any better and no one else would fix my feelings of loss.

I experienced many tower moments. At first, I got trapped in thoughts of "Why didn't I know this?" or "Why didn't I know that?" The truth is I knew what I knew when I knew it. There is no other way. Moving beyond this required that I accept the role of my ignorance as the catalyst for the tower moment. Each tower was supposed to happen and brought me closer to my rightful path.

At the time, this was hard to see. Instead, I discounted tower moments as coincidental or attributed them to karmic reparations. It was difficult to recognize that these moments resulted from actions I took. I stopped blaming myself once I recognized my agency.

Unfortunately, no one explained this to me. I probably would not have heeded the advice anyway. My ego was so fragile and damaged that I really thought I understood what was unfolding in my life. Yet, the more I pushed against my own healing, the more challenging things got. The more I began to uncover, the more I realized I was unaware of what this tower moment was preparing me for.

These tower moments forced me to dig deeper. When I moved away from blaming others, I found parts of myself that I didn't know were buried. The work was challenging but it also allowed me to make peace with myself and build myself up to the next level of consciousness. Blame dissipated once I realized that this was an opportunity to evolve into a better version of myself. Redefining each transformational moment as an opportunity to grow and learn was the only way to move forward. I started to see that I was walking in the right direction toward my purpose.

Tower moments brought me to a place of vulnerability, a place where I knew I could not go one more day with such upheaval. The tower reminded me that choices exist in a delicate balance of success and failure, more and less, happiness and sadness. I needed to embrace that any experience I engaged in was not an accident. Each leg of the journey includes a culminating project or challenge. These are moments where we are given the opportunity to demonstrate what we have learned to this point. During the tower moment, I didn't recognize that I needed to prepare for the culminating challenge. Yet, the strange reality was that I was preparing the whole time. Though unaware of it, each experience led me to another pearl of wisdom. Instead of seeing it, I ignored it and I ran from the crossroad.

Looking back, my advice to myself would be "lean in." When I fought back, there was chaos and I spiraled deeper into depression. When I was on the correct path, I asked myself "What am I here to do? How can I most impact the world?" I had to harness my sense of knowing, to sense the path that resonated with my soul journey.

I engaged so deeply in this work that I began to resolve childhood issues. I freed myself from self-imposed chains by realizing that my father's death had nothing to do with me. He was sick and he fought as hard as he could until the end. As a child I could not know that it was his time. Instead, I personalized it and thought about many "what ifs" that may have changed the outcome. As an adult, I finally saw there was nothing that I could have done.

I leaned into the notion that not all experiences will be what I wanted them to be. I released blame and I accepted that we all have a predestined purpose. As I walked the path to finding my "soul purpose," I discovered that it was beautiful and incredible.

Guiding Questions:

1. What role did you play in your current condition?

2. How do your circumstances change if you blame yourself or someone else?

Chapter 4
The Lie: Are You Worthy?

Before this tower moment, much of my past was based on my faulty perception of my own value. I spent years measuring my worth based on what and how much I produced. I struggled to recognize that I connected material wealth with success. My self-value was predicated on how or if others thought I had value. In my subconscious, I connected that external value with wealth. This connection between material wealth and success came from my childhood and societal conditioning. Growing up, I attended private schools and the children I went to school with came from very wealthy families. I did not. The message was the more money your family had, the more important you were. Those students made sure I knew that I came from a home with less. That I was less. Through this experience, I associated money with being seen and being valued.

I was trapped in an exhausting mental Olympics trying to show others (and myself) that I made it, that I was smart enough, successful enough... as if status was the gauge of importance or value. I had based my values on faulty belief systems, focusing on what was easily seen by the outside world. I spent years of my life competing with others to showcase how great I was. The critical question to avoid this trap was "what do I truly value?" I was stopped dead in my tracks by the words of David Goggins, whose book pushed me to change course: "glossy surfaces reflect far more than they reveal." (Goggins p.15) His powerful statement reminded me that my true power and beauty were below the glossy surface of the material world and, so far, I was failing to see them.

I struggled because there was something undone within me, distorting my self-view. To break through that glossy surface, I needed to identify the lies that held me back. I could only understand how I associated my worth and values with non-truths once I was fully engaged in the self-reflection and healing process. As I examined the doubts, fears, and anxieties that often guided my decisions, I gained clarity around the actions I took that did not serve me well. Underlying those actions and decisions was an identifiable belief that limited my success, a lie I told myself about my worth or capability. I needed to stop and consider what choice or action led me here, what lie or limiting belief led to that choice or action? I had a mental tape on repeat when I faced a challenge: I couldn't do it; I wasn't worthy; I wasn't enough. I still hear the tape sometimes, but now I know the negative thoughts are a lie.

I worked to fully understand the damage of the lies that made me feel unworthy and to move beyond my limited thinking. I focused on how I perceived myself and this intentional reflection allowed me to move forward through my healing processes.

As I began doing some genuine reflection, I started to realize I was merely existing. The lie convinced me to accept a substandard existence. It limited my perspective, growth, and ability to expand. And so, I contracted. I wrongly accepted there was nothing more to gain or enjoy. Up until that point, I was ok with mediocrity. Receiving "kind of what I needed" was good enough.

My heart failed to be illuminated, grew comfortable with the numb feeling that invaded my body. Feeding the lie allowed me to minimize my light and embrace a feeling of emotional unavailability. I could feel that I was not able to connect deeply with people, yet I believed that I was emotionally available. I know now that I was in denial.

Looking back on the loss of my relationship, I understand why it was easier to believe the lie that I was not worthy than it was to do the work to learn the truth. I told myself that lie for so long that it was all I knew. Even if someone had told me the work would propel me to spiritual freedom, I would have told them they were wrong. As long as I was lost in the appearance of happiness or was attempting to capture it through someone else's eyes, the lie grew bigger. But the lie could only exist if I continued to buy into it and feed it.

The stakes were high. I tended to feed the lie of unworthiness through my thoughts and actions. The metaphorical poison I put in my mind and body helped distract me from the truth that I was more powerful than comprehension. If I did not arrive at an understanding that uncovering the lie was part of my journey, I would never reach a true understanding about who I was and the immense value I brought to this world.

Our society teaches you that if you are not wealthy, you are not worthy. It's everywhere; you must drive the nicest car, live in the largest house, and wear the most expensive name brand of clothing to be a worthy and valued part of your community.

As I learned this message growing up, I bought into it. I know there are so many of us in the world that have attached our worth to material items as a way of trying to fill the hole in our hearts. The truth is each of us is uniquely special with so much to offer. We must do this work to understand that the people around us love us and want us as we are. If we don't know our worth, we will create space around us that teaches people the only way to love us is to ask us what we can do for them.

When I reflect on raising my children, I feel a sense of sadness for the time that I did not maximize. I did not understand that my presence in their life was more important to them than the material things I bought or provided. I believed that my job as a parent was to provide them the material things in life. In doing that, I neglected to equally share myself with them. Don't get me wrong, I was there on weekends, birthdays, parent/teacher conferences etc. but generally I spent much of my time working as a principal at a school. Interestingly enough, this truth was shared with me by my youngest son. One day we were talking about his and his brother's upbringing. He shared that they knew that my job required me to work a lot. He spoke about how they would look forward to the weekends because they knew that was when they would have my time. Crazy enough, by the time we had this conversation, I had started to recognize this pattern and knew exactly what he was talking about.

This raw, open dialogue with my son may seem awkward and riddled with conflict but know that it was had with much love and was a true inflection point in my life. Hearing him made my heart hurt as I felt like not only had I let them down, but that time had expired because they were grown. I listened and could feel my heart beating fast, realizing that during that time, I did not have any self-esteem. I believed that giving things was a real way of expressing love and that became the way people engaged with me. The funny part is that once I inadvertently created those parameters for engagement, I became angry and frustrated at people who would seek me out to serve in that capacity. In retrospect, I taught those around me that I was only useful and available as a monetary support and then I got mad when they treated me as such. I bring this up because many of us create situations based on how we feel about ourselves and then, as we evolve, we struggle to accept how we set up the circumstance, and ultimately, are challenged to create new boundaries and ways of engaging. I explained to my son, as we had that insightful conversation, that in that time in my life, unfortunately, I did not know that I was enough. In that space, I realized that even though I was successful in the world's eye, I struggled to understand that I had worth and value even with nothing. That I, alone, am priceless.

That tower moment was meant for me but when I first encountered a tower moment, I couldn't see what was best for me. It was meant to teach me and free me from myself. Sometimes my needs outweighed my wants and my wants were not always in my best interest. I often dreamed or created visions that I believed I wanted yet failed to recognize that they may be detrimental to achieving my dreams and goals. Any time I became distracted, it derailed me from moving in the direction of my life's purpose.

My life journey shifts based on the decisions I make. One decision may unlock a completely different set of situations to face to reach my soul purpose. I create my experience through how I choose to travel the road. In tower moments, the universe gives us incredible opportunities to grow from challenge. I had the power to decide what type of growth I gained from them. Tower moments were there to assist me in evolving to my best self.

Once I made meaning of my tower moment, I was able to share my truth as it relates to my "soul purpose."

I could then help others make meaning of their own moments. My ability to speak freely, candidly, and compassionately about my experiences supported others to examine their own experiences and contextualize tower moments as moments of growth.

Tower moments build our emotional capacity to see beyond what is. Deconstructing tower moments helped me navigate and understand them and support others through the process. To support those needing healing, I had to start the journey to my own healing.

My soul purpose is intricately linked to raising the vibration of the world. This can only be achieved by living in love, empathy, and compassion. Without dealing with my emotional baggage, I could not genuinely give or receive love; how then could I accomplish my true-life mission? How could I walk gracefully with those attributes without being able to feel them authentically? How could I heal others without first healing myself? How could I empathize with others if I had not experienced pain and loss?

Everything I needed to persevere was already within me, but I couldn't see that. I had been training for this tower moment much of my life, but I needed to be able to give in to the experience. Investigating the tower takes time, intentional exploration, and patience.

Guiding Questions:

1. What is the connection between being successful and being enough?

2. What does success mean to you?

3. In what ways are you enough?

4. What beliefs about your worth negatively impact the way you engage with the world?

5. How are these beliefs a barrier to achieving your goals?

4

The Lie: Are You Worthy?

Chapter 5
The Truth: More Powerful Than Comprehension

As I peeled back the layers of my lies, I saw the harm I caused myself and, in some cases, others because I was scared to see my worth and potential. I started to walk my path and uncover my capabilities: I was more powerful than comprehension and so are you. We each are here to do something, but our unawareness gets in the way. I started to recognize that I had the power within myself. I reflected on the times that I felt I had to shrink myself to fit into someone else's narrow belief system. Any situation that leaves you feeling as if you need to shrink yourself is not for your highest good.

When thinking of being more powerful than comprehension, I think about the ways we take back our power to reclaim self. Truthfully that looks very different depending on who we are. That moment can come to fruition through leaving a job, moving away from relationships, standing up for yourself, etc.

For me, this moment came when I decided to leave a job. This was a job that many strive to achieve. It had a fancy title and good money attached to it. I was on the path of climbing the career ladder to the next level. Additionally, if I would have stayed several more years, it provided the comfort of safety and came with a great pension. I share all the attributes of the job because that is how I, and others, would describe it. I share this because, while I recognized all it came with, I simultaneously can recall my unhappiness in that role. I would spend much time sitting in the feeling of dissatisfaction. At some point, I remember realizing that it was not the job I thought it would be. I thought this position would enable me to effectuate change. It did not. Instead, I stumbled upon the contrary. It closed me off from the things that mattered most to me — children. While I thought taking the job would provide an opportunity for me to make change, instead it felt like I was shrinking. My dreams were getting smaller, my excitement waned, the joy had left my eyes, and I felt powerless. There were multiple reasons why I felt this way. Some of the reasons were grounded in feeling unseen, which made me feel ineffective. Some were connected to a fundamental feeling of unfulfillment due to feelings of lack of progress. Some were grounded in feeling like I became the face of something but had no actual power to make changes.

I struggled because I thought I was stuck. It kind of felt like walking too far down a road and thinking that

The Truth: More Powerful Than Comprehension

it was too late to turn back. I felt bound even though I was free. Part of being bound was connected to thinking I was letting people down if I walked away. By staying I was letting myself down. I concluded that I had all that I needed to free myself by walking away. There was nothing and no one holding me anywhere but me. Fear was the only thing holding me back. Taking back my power looked like walking away from the comfort, the title, and the money.

Considering this, I knew that I needed to leave. Summoning my courage, I started to think about what was going to come next. What I knew for sure was that I wanted a job that brought joy, helped me live in my purpose, and provided me an opportunity to find my own agency. Without being completely sure how that next role would provide that – I stepped out of safety and walked into faith.

True growth involves expansion. I grew outward and inward. As this process unfolded, I questioned why it had taken so long to realize the gifts I can bring to the world. For me to expand, I needed to understand both what my gifts were and how to use them effectively. They were revealed when I was ready to understand them.

As in a video game, it was impossible to unlock the next level until the current one was mastered. I could not go to the next level of self-learning until I mastered all the lessons of the current level. Each level gave me the information necessary to become successful. When the time was right, I gained access to the next level of my journey.

Each transformational moment tested me to see if I was ready to unlock the next level. The universe watched to see if my actions matched my words. Until they did, I received lessons, challenges, and surprises – opportunities for my actions to reflect my words. When they did not, I would repeat. When they matched, I continued to move forward.

Once I could live my truth, I was ready. My most important mission in life was to learn to love unconditionally. This could not occur until I learned to love myself with the same level of commitment and dedication I offered others. Acknowledging that I was more powerful than comprehension required me to take care of myself — mind, body, and spirit. If I did not nurture and care for all three aspects of my wholeness, I was not ready. When I nurtured my mind, I was a careful consumer of what I ingested intellectually. I ensured that the information I took in pushed my thinking, empowered me towards continued improvement, and expanded my knowledge base. When I loved my body, I treated it kindly, balancing myself with proper rest, healthy food, and consistent exercise. Nurturing my spirit required me to remain attuned with nature, understand energy as fluid, and continually seek what lay beyond the logical. I began to accept that much of what I experienced did not have logical outcomes. I needed to find comfort in knowing that a higher power always guided me towards true abundance.

Many of us struggle to acknowledge that we matter and have value. Coming to terms with my own self-worth enabled me to authentically show up as myself and offer more to others. We each must recognize that we are deserving. When I began to uncover the truth about my value, worth, intellect, and ability, I paused in awe, realizing that everyone is on Earth for a unique purpose. I felt reborn when I experienced the freedom to express and harness my strengths and to appreciate how my power could impact the world. I was excited by the possibilities. I felt like a fawn I once saw. Testing its legs, it began jumping around in a small pond: overcome by the newfound power of its legs, it decided to live fully in freedom and began romping around the yard. What a beautiful moment, as the fawn truly lived in the power of its body and spirit!

Acknowledging and accepting that I had a purpose — to impact the world positively — was liberating. Within me, I had what was necessary to be successful. I would sit for hours and ponder these questions, allowing my thoughts to flow freely:

- How do I currently impact the world?

- How are my truth and my purpose in the world linked?

As I reflected deeply, I would not judge my thoughts. I would write my thoughts down and try to assess where I found truth and where I found lies.

What I was attempting to unlock was the knowledge of my gifts. I began to realize that we all have strengths we don't recognize, and that we each possess infinite potential. For me, those strengths included being authentically empathetic, being able to connect with people and support them to find their best self, and listening long enough to hear what they needed. I was awakening to the fact that my placement in the world was not accidental. I had a life purpose and finding it was essential to contribute to the world in the most impactful way. Imagine the world we would live in if we all realized our gifts.

What I uncovered during this phase of my tower cycle was that I had seen glimpses of my own greatness throughout my life, but I was unable to believe what had been shown to me. This part of the process allowed me to dig beneath the surface. I not only saw my greatness but I finally acknowledged it. My power was needed. I was moved to impact the world to a greater extent. I realized that the truth was not only for me but also for the world, which was made brighter as I offered my light. Even writing this book, I struggled to acknowledge my power. I had to realize that it does not diminish anyone else's power. We must each discover our own gifts and that will change the world. The inability to do so reinforces the lie that we are not transformational beings.

Guiding Questions:

1. How can you recognize the gifts you bring into the world?

2. How are you more powerful than comprehension?

5

The Truth: More Powerful Than Comprehension

Chapter 6
What's at Stake: Finding Freedom

Everyone experiences these cyclical tower moments throughout their lives. They occur to remind us that we have something very valuable to accomplish here on earth. Because tower moments generally accompany much upheaval, it can be difficult to see how they can lead us to uncovering our truths. Seeing the connection between individual events and understanding how those events collectively push us enables us to find deeper awareness that we have something great to accomplish here. Our role in creating change in the world is defined by our willingness to explore our tower moments and how each leads to another aspect of our growth. While it would have been easier not to seek deeper meaning from my tower experience, this was a key moment to realize my truest power and embrace life.

At this point, I was knee deep in the tower experience. It was tough. While I consider myself to be reasonably insightful, I reflected that I had failed to truly process childhood experiences. Throughout my life, I had often looked back to assess my growth, but now I felt that I'd fallen short. I had not been able to make the connections. As I pieced together episodes from my life, I suddenly understood that they were not coincidental.

I started to understand, in a very profound way, what this experience was offering me. During this time, I focused a lot on the possible outcomes if I remained stuck in a place of fear. I risked staying in the same place, unaware of my power, unable to reach my true purpose. I realized I could not live the life I wanted and deserved if I was unwilling to honestly look at the choices that lead me here, to this moment. Exploring what was at stake highlighted what I would lose if I didn't take a chance on the opportunity to grow.

I recognized how I ignored my soul purpose. I believed that I was meant to live in the shadow of others. Many of us are so focused on what we think we want that we neglect to consider our purpose may be bigger than our own vision or comprehension. First, I had to cultivate the capacity to dream bigger.

What was at stake was my mental, emotional, and spiritual freedom. I recognized that if I didn't take time to look inward, it would be difficult to move past this moment to the next stage of my life. What was at stake was a deeper understanding of who I was, what I came to this world to do, and how I could use my gifts. What was at stake was the idea that I was meant to do something extraordinary: my potential to raise the vibration of the world by helping individuals love the broken pieces of themselves. The only path toward my true purpose was to craft my own vision, make my own meaning, and reach my own goals.

Up until this point, I looked at this tower moment as something happening to me instead of an opportunity. When I realized what was at stake, I began to think about the ways I could investigate my tower moment and myself a little bit deeper to understand my true purpose. While I could not see the whole picture, I knew it was necessary: my intuition was guiding me to a space of self-understanding.

I could not run away from this situation and realized that working through this cycle would allow me to reclaim something that I had clearly lost. I had worked hard to get to a place of material comfort, but, when I got there, I no longer recognized myself. I could have all the material success I was looking for, but it wasn't enough. This was an opportunity to find peace of mind and calm of spirit. I took this opportunity to find myself.

It is my hope that this chapter will help you come to terms with and make meaning of what is at stake for you. Don't let this moment pass you by.

Guiding Questions:

1. Why are you not currently living the life you want to live?

2. What is at stake if you allow yourself to remain stuck?

3. What outcomes may grow out of embracing the potential of tower moments?

4. How can these lessons help you live in alignment with your soul purpose?

6

What's at Stake: Finding Freedom

Chapter 7
Face Your Fears: You vs. You

I knew I was approaching the end of this tower moment when I brought a different perspective to the issues that plagued me. No longer seeking to blame, no longer being harsh with myself, understanding that this moment had a place in the journey of who I ultimately hope to be. These changes signaled progress and evolution. When I rushed to find the answers, when I failed to sit in the moments and feel my emotions, I was forced to face the lesson again and again. I suffered enormous frustration when repeating these lessons. Reflecting on that frustration, I realized by taking my time reaching the end, I did not have to re-experience the lessons.

Each part of my evolution was crucial. The smallest realization was an essential piece in reaching my potential. There was no quick way. As with running a marathon, the preparation takes a lot of dedication and commitment. You may be tempted to skip the full process of training but if you do, you will not be prepared; you will not have the skills or the stamina; you may not even be sure why you're still running. When race day comes, you might start off with a group of runners but as you hit your limits, you may be tempted to drop out, or worse, hail a cab. You might arrive at the finish line but you will know you did not do the work. The universe can see if you take the cab. It will put you in another similar situation and this time there won't be a shortcut. Without the training, you will be unprepared for the future. Eventually, you'll have to go back to the beginning to finish. If you take your time to do the work, it won't be a short cut, but it will be shorter than repeating the cycle again and again.

During this cycle, there were times when I believed I had learned all I needed to learn. The universe continued to send different challenges my way to test my resolve. When presented with a test, an opportunity to demonstrate that I had indeed learned from the past, I failed. For example, I had disconnected from engaging in relationships that felt unhealthy. Spending time in dysfunctional relational patterns with others was harmful to my wellbeing and being around them reinforced that I was not worthy of love. Many times, it is easier to believe that we are unworthy than to step into the fact that we are worthy. The closer I got to realizing my worth and stepping into purpose, the more invitations I received to engage in distractions and detours. Until I was able to stand in my worth and set boundaries with these relationships, I would continue to be dragged down by those who did not value me or help me to get to my highest good.

7

Face Your Fears: You vs. You

As we move through the process of evolving to our best selves, our readiness and commitment will be tested. These tests may come in many forms. The more healing I engaged in, the more challenges tested my resolve to move past the pain and into a healthier space. These challenges appeared disguised as opportunities: higher job titles that did not align with where I wanted to go and relationships with people whose values no longer aligned with mine. The closer I got to the top of an organization, the more I was asked to sacrifice my ideals and integrity. It was my job to retain clarity and recognize them as challenges. My grandmother often reminded me, "all that glitters is not gold" but my instinct was to let glitter distract me. I realized that I did not need what I thought I needed. Finally, I recognized that aligning my words to my actions was what gave me a sense of purpose and worth. The reappearance of these challenges signified that I was at the tail end of this chapter of my learning. I had already begun to move beyond the past, and though it was ok to occasionally look back, I needed to keep moving forward.

This is when we must face our fears. To do that, we need to identify what it is we are afraid of. Are we afraid of being alone, not being successful, not being financially stable, not finding our true purpose? Many times, our fears get in the way and keep us stuck. We tend to stick with what we know, even if it does not serve us.

Facing your fears is about taking the risk to walk towards discomfort. Facing your fears is all about doing what comes naturally which is counter to popular culture. It's ok to live your own life and walk your own path, but that is counter to societal messages that connect to the matrix. The tension exists between building your own vision or conforming to someone else's vision of who you need to be.

Is there anything in your life that you wanted to do but didn't because you were afraid to fail? I ask that, knowing that I was in the same place as you. The best example that I can share is the thought of writing this book. I knew that it was something that I was led to do. Yet, I spent much time during the writing process engaging in negative self-talk. Sometimes the inner voice inside my mind would get loud. Often, I would hear "you cannot do it" or "you are wasting your time." Those thoughts filled me with anxiety which would paralyze my progress. Many days and nights I had to reach deep within to recognize the thoughts. When the voices in your mind are that loud, it is because you are close to creating something that will make a difference. My fear was sometimes centered around worrying about failure. The truth for me was that it would only be a failure if I didn't try.

Rushing through healing and evolution is counterproductive. Fortunately, there is no deadline for completion. It is less important to complete the cycle than to intentionally meander, investigate, and discover where you're going. Slow down; reflect on the journey.

Once I reached this stage in the process, I could take a big breath. This tower moment was the first time in my life that I was forced to take time with myself. It took time to see beyond the surface of my life experience.

7

Face Your Fears: You vs. You

The experience was a call to grow more deeply than ever before, to awaken to my potential, and to embrace my future. With introspection, I looked back on the journey as an observer and took time to marvel at my progress. I had gone inward to explore the pieces of me that were undone and now I was almost there.

Each experience, particularly each tower moment, is meant to teach you something about achieving true purpose. The learning exists between experiencing the tower and making meaning of it. Surviving this middle passage was essential to genuinely understanding where I had arrived. The middle passage is the place to reflect, investigate, and learn from the tower moment. It is the time and space you give yourself.

It was the first moment I became aware that my future was brighter than I ever could have dreamed; when I saw that what I prayed for or had desired was nothing compared to what I deserved. Unburdening fear requires shining light into shadows. Looking at your fears quickly as you run by is not the same as shining light on them, observing them, befriending them. Treat the child inside the way you would treat a child afraid of a monster under the bed – even if you're an adult, even if you "shouldn't" be afraid. Use kind, gentle, nurturing and forgiving hands.

As I moved through my journey, the version of myself that I left behind was almost unrecognizable. I started to understand my purpose and how I could use my intellect and ability to positively contribute to the world. My perspective shifted from "why is this happening to me" to "this is happening for me." I learned that my voice was valuable and that it was imperative that I use it in constructive ways. As I found and valued myself, the fear I had of being heard, valued, and appreciated started to leave. I began to love the pieces of me that I had loathed in the past.

Guiding Questions:

1. What moments in life challenge your growth?

2. How can you prepare to face your fears as you arrive at the end of this tower moment?

7
Face Your Fears: You vs. You

Chapter 8
Surrender to the Outcome

Initially, I didn't want to accept that these tower moments were opportunities to learn and grow. Honestly, I had no clue there were meanings or lessons connected to them. While we often look for meaning as to why things happen to us, it can be very difficult to process when the events are negative. Recognizing that each tower moment was indicative of certain patterns or themes in my life was truly an opportunity to progress to the next level of my evolution. Growth can be frustrating – especially when you have an outcome in mind. In my life, I strongly believed that there were certain outcomes that I deserved. My need to focus on the destination caused me to struggle and made it more difficult to see the lessons. By making meaning of this tower moment and processing it, I realized that what I wanted and focused on wasn't where I needed or was meant to go. In retrospect, it is not my job to decree the outcome.

Surrendering to the outcome is extremely difficult. It requires letting go of dictating what the outcome "should" be. You choose what to plant, you help keep it healthy, but, ultimately, the plant needs to grow a certain way — it grows through its relationship to the sun. Surrendering to the outcome requires humility; it requires recognizing that the universe is directing you toward your sun – your soul purpose, whether you can see that light yet or not. It's about letting go. When I finally gained an understanding of the purpose of the journey, I could let go of the journey's outcome and, along with it, the pain.

When I understood the purpose of my life journey was to realize my fullest potential, I stopped focusing on the outcomes and spent more time in the present, processing my experiences, figuring out what steps I should take and how those steps influenced my life. The mistake I had made was believing that I could dictate the destination. Instead, I started to figure out how I wanted to move forward. I began to think through how I wanted to feel and behave when I got there – wherever there was.

My advice for surrendering to the outcome is to focus on how you want to feel. What makes you smile? What brings joy to your heart? Focusing on these may help align you and bring true abundance to fruition.

I acknowledged that I had worked hard to get through tough circumstances and embarked on deep self-learning. I learned a tremendous amount about myself. I had done an incredible amount of soul-searching and, as a result, I had planted many seeds that would

Surrender to the Outcome

eventually grow into abundance. I believed and had faith that what I deserved was coming.

Realizing and accepting that the universe has a divine plan for each of us allowed me to relinquish control and surrender to the outcome. It was incumbent upon me to make decisions that brought me closer to manifesting my abundance through reaching my life purpose. Embracing tower moments as part of the cycle of growth, as opportunities to bring me closer to my best self, showed me that the best-case scenario in my mind fell short of what I deserved. Figuring out how to lean into the change was part of the challenge. When I surrendered to the outcome, I realized that the next part of my journey was near.

Over the course of this tower moment, I had sown many seeds of change, growth, and evolution. When I surrendered to the outcome, I realized that I had done all the work necessary to reap what I'd sown. While I was nowhere near done learning, growing, and evolving, I had done enough to reach the rewards of this part of the journey. Finally, I had faith that I'd done enough, contributed enough, that I was enough. It is always important to look back, reflect, and celebrate how far you have come on your journey.

Guiding Question:

1. How can you surrender to the outcome without defining the destination?

2. What ways can you affirm for yourself that you are already enough?

Chapter 9
Rise as the Phoenix

Welcome to this celebratory chapter! Whether you're arriving at this point alongside me, or you are still working to get here, I want you to reflect on all you have already accomplished. Wherever you are in your journey, your phoenix will rise.

For me, this is the most important chapter because it's about the moment where the pain subsides, the voices get quieter, and you start to feel your actual power. That moment came for me a few years ago while I was preparing a keynote presentation for my current employer. The night before the presentation, I spent time on the phone rehashing a painful situation and trying to work through it. It didn't go the way I hoped it would by facing it, addressing it, and letting it go. That night, I remember crying myself to sleep because I knew that the time had come to close that chapter in my life. In that moment, I was beyond exhausted and so very angry. All I knew was the next day I had to get up and present to a standing-room-only crowd. It seemed impossible.

My sleep was troubled; I was unable to get the deep sleep I so desperately needed. When I woke up the next morning, I somehow managed to get out of bed, get dressed and leave to meet up with my coworkers. I remember walking around with them feeling lost and numb. One of my colleagues has this way of reminding you of your power in the moments that you forget it. On that day, her impact was particularly important and she didn't even know that her words were breathing life into a person who was so exhausted and so broken.

The time to present the keynote came. I was sitting in the back of the room, ready to go up and deliver the keynote on "*Seeding the Soul of Change.*" I was speaking to what should've been a full room of women, about harnessing who we could truly be if we understood the ways in which the world dictates to us who we should be. To my surprise, men entered the room. It dawned on me that what I was saying was resonating with men as well. I realized it was a conversation about everyone's life. I realized that what I was saying was not gender specific but instead universal.

I spoke to them about their power as transformational leaders and as people who are in spaces to create change.

9
Rise as the Phoenix

Suddenly it hit me. In the process of sharing this keynote with them I realized that I was talking to myself as a woman who was occupying space, who was there to create change. In that moment the Phoenix rose from the ashes! In that moment, kind of like an "aha" moment if you will, I understood that I had made it! Not only had I gotten up and gotten ready to do what had seemed an impossibility the night before, but I was absolutely accomplishing what I had set out to do and recognized that I had the power to find my center. I understood, without any doubts, that I could share my message with people and simultaneously fill myself and remind myself of my obligation to myself. So next time you are unsure of yourself, remember your power, your strength, and your value!

Each tower moment has a purpose. Looking back, I see that my tower moment occurred to provoke self-investigation. When we make sense of our tower moments, we realize they occur cyclically. Each cycle of transformational growth is meant to move us to the next part of our life journey.

I navigated through this cycle by taking the time to be introspective. I learned that while I could speak, my ability to communicate was stifled. I wanted to place blame but realized that it's about the learning, not the blame. As I began to gain perspective, I realized that I was holding onto ways of being that trapped me in lies and limited the way I traveled along my journey. I unearthed and faced lies connected to doubt, fear, worth, and value that have lived within me for most of my life. I interrogated and perhaps interrupted the lies. I gained understanding about how they were reinforced throughout my life. I realized that these lies left me feeling unworthy and devalued, causing me to question if I was enough. This was the beginning of understanding my life's purpose.

Part of this journey was to understand my own power, realize my own strength, and work to find the next best version of myself. I wrestled with concepts of self-worth and community. I started to think about what type of relationships and energy I wanted to be surrounded by and what I was able to offer to those in my life. It is not just about having others pour into you but how we show up and give back to those in our day-to-day exchanges. Now, I see my value and worth in the world. In seeing those qualities, I can recognize that every one of us is imperfectly perfect. Within that imperfection is beauty. I now understand that I have much that I can contribute to the world, but, more importantly, I understand how every single human around me has much to contribute to the world as well.

I moved to a place of self-love. I recognized how complex life is and began to awaken to the truth. My shift changed the way I interacted with people and the way they interacted with me. My transformational moment unlocked different pieces of myself that I didn't know existed or forgot I had. I had been blind to the fact that I was destined to raise the vibration of humanity through my contributions. I was transformational in nature and so are you. Each of us have a special purpose here on earth and it is essential that you uncover and unlock your purpose. Now, I can acknowledge that I am more powerful than comprehension. That we each are more powerful than comprehension. I understand the need to love myself.

It is necessary to recognize our own true worth to create change. To do so, we must recognize what is at stake, what is necessary to sacrifice, and the abundance we would receive if we were willing to take this opportunity to look within ourselves.

The transformational nature of this cycle was meant to bring me closer to finding my "soul purpose." I endured, experienced, learned, lost, and overcame. I embraced my worth, and uncovered the lesson that tower moments can be opportunities for us to grow. This tower moment shifted how I saw the world and it helped me to see that sharing this knowledge might help others on their journey as well.

At the end of this transformational cycle, I recognized how to harness the lessons I learned. I realized what was necessary in terms of truth, guidance, and learning to inform my next steps. I figured out what tools I should use and how I should use them to inform my practice. I have started to make decisions that are best for me. The closer I get to understanding who I am, the closer I am to nearing the end of this transformational cycle.

A reckoning has occurred. I will continue to be tested, challenged with opportunities to face my fears. As I evolve, I am better able to recognize when my fears are reappearing. When presented with the past, I lean into what I have learned about myself and observe the fears for what they are. I try not to waver because I try not to allow doubt and fear to enter my realm. To be clear, fear and doubt didn't leave my life, but now I process their purpose differently. Now, when fear and doubt creep into my mind, I reflect knowing that those emotions are pushing me to find the root cause. I smile, reflecting on the difference in my thoughts and actions from before this tower moment. I am ready to celebrate the ending of this transformational cycle.

Each time I engage in this process of investigation, I become more attuned to the possibilities of life, better able to experience it with joy and deepen my understanding that there can be no progress without struggle.

The process has humbled me in a way I could never have ever imagined. I realize that I am always growing and evolving. There are battles I have fought recently that I could not have survived at a different stage in my life because I was not prepared. This stage helped me contextualize that there are no accidents or coincidences. EVERY experience I have is divinely orchestrated. Once I can understand and acquiesce, I better situate myself to open to my fullest potential and receive abundance.

One of the most important truths gained on this path is knowing that I can do it: I can heal and grow and be ok. Even though this stage has been painful, it has awakened a better, stronger, and wiser version of me. As I rise from the ashes, I realize that the pain was temporary, but the learning was limitless.

I view the world differently now. Actually, the world looks differently at me too! This stage is tricky, because I feel victorious — and I am — however, this cycle of growth is one of many cycles along my path. Each cycle awakens another part of my and your destiny. There are still parts of me that are broken, as I am imperfectly perfect. I revisit this process in each chapter of my life. As I continue to evolve, I am better prepared to do the next level of work, always moving closer to where I need to be. I surrender to the outcome, knowing that what comes next is not something that I can control. Instead, I ponder the aspects of what I want to come next. I think about how I want to feel as I move forward.

Working through my tower moment provided an opportunity to stand in my greatness — a rising of the phoenix moment. As the phoenix, I gained the perspective that life is not happening to me but happening with me. This process helped me find my way back to my true self and to embrace that I am perfectly imperfect — as is everyone else.

The rising of the phoenix symbolizes not an end point but an evolution. Now is the time to ascend to the next level. In order to do so, you must harness the skills and tools you acquired on this journey. Within you, you possess all that's necessary to undertake this next journey in life.

Guiding Questions:

1. When you look back on your journey, what do you appreciate?

2. What mental and emotional strength did you require to get to this part of the journey?

9
Rise as the Phoenix

Congratulations: you rose to the occasion! You have conquered some of your past and made connections to the lies that you have held firmly about yourself. You have walked through the fire and come out the other side stronger and wiser. You stand before the world, arms outstretched, marveling at your victory. You can now look at the world through the fresh lens of the next level of awakening.

There will be more tower moments throughout your life. Now you are prepared to experience them from a different perspective. You are strong enough to persevere through each of them to achieve your next level of awareness.

Emerging from the tower moment, you are ready to stand in your conviction and realize your value, your worth, and most importantly your gifts. Standing strong among the rubble of false foundations, you are still here. Scars of beauty, strength, resolve, and conviction. You are reborn as a stronger, wiser, more grounded, and intuitive self. You are witness to and observer of your own success and devotion to your purpose. You were divinely guided to your path. Grasp the magic of faith and wisdom.

You are the phoenix...........It is your time to RISE!

Acts of Liberation

Acknowledgements

This book would not have come to fruition without the love, support, wisdom, and encouragement from so many people. I want to express my deepest gratitude for all of those who poured into me and this book.

First and foremost, I want to thank God for choosing and using me as a vessel to share these words with the world.

I want to thank the team at Kaleidoscope Vibrations for your unwavering support. Yael R. Rosenstock Gonzalez, I am eternally grateful for the team you put together to bring this book to life. Thank you for your belief in this project and its potential impact on the world.

Katherine Kolios — It is difficult to put into words how much you brought to this project. Your unyielding faith in what this book could be supported me to revisit the best ways to lift-up its message. I am forever indebted to you for your honest, candid, and loving feedback. Thank you so much for the gentle push to lean into my authenticity.

Logic Thompson — Your illustrations make my words come to life. It is through your eyes that I see the struggle, the strength, and the beauty of transformation.

Caroline Rinaldy — I am forever grateful for your perpetual flexibility in bringing all of this book's components into a beautiful masterpiece. Your keen sense of how each word lives on a page is masterful.

Ed — You are always there. During the best and most challenging times, you always provide me comfort. Thank you for always believing in me and being my brother. I am forever grateful for your presence in my life.

Logan — You are one of my greatest masterpieces. You are so kind and loving but fearless in how you show up in the world. Thank you for the countless times you would call and say, "Eb, how's the book going?" Know that your words were always a gentle reminder of my responsibility to myself. Thank you for always showing up to love even the imperfect pieces of me.

Amy — What can I say? You are a gift, and I am so blessed to have you by my side. I have learned so much from you. With you, I have learned to be fearless in the pursuit of my dreams, patient in understanding the complexity of my progress, and proud of who I have become. Your unwavering belief in how I can impact the world has been life altering. Thank you for listening to my endless chatter about this book and for sitting with me nights on end, encouraging me to continue to finish.

Acknowledgements

Maria — Thank you for all of the calls and meetings to chat about the book. Thank you for reading and re-reading each time I called you. Thank you helping me to plan, build, and dream bigger. I am forever grateful for your contribution.

Deb J — You are always there for me. Thank you for your mentorship and love throughout this process. Thank you for the countless times you encouraged me to keep going and to believe in myself.

Tina V — Thank you for all your love and guidance along my path. You continually remind me that I have more to do in this world. Your guidance has been priceless.

Sybil — Thank you for the brainstorming sessions. Thank you for the push to keep going even when it gets tough. I'm super blessed to have you as part of my soul family.

Dynell K, Hewette M, and Nate D — Your influence during the writing of this book has been monumental. I know that none of you was aware that I was in a space of healing; yet, the impact that your compassion, encouragement and nurturing spirits had on the birth of this beautiful book is immeasurable.

Robin C – You taught me far more than you know. You taught me to lead through a compassionate lens. Thank you for believing in the possibility of who I could be even when I could not see it myself.

Acts of Liberation

To all of the family and friends I was unable to specifically name here — Thank you for every conversation, every laugh, every moment that you have reminded me of my responsibility to myself. You have influenced my existence in ways that I could never appropriately put into words. I appreciate and value each and every one of you. With much gratitude; I love you dearly.

About the Author

Dr. Ebony Green is a seasoned educator who has spent much of her life working to improve the quality of education for children within the K-12 system. A teacher, administrator, executive director of equity and access, public speaker, and author, she has worked hard to address the needs of the underrepresented and is dedicated to the pursuit of creating a more socially just world. A renowned public speaker, Dr. Green is known to present to standing room only and leaves her audience wanting more. She has an amazing ability to gently push her listeners to examine how their experiences shape their beliefs. Dr. Green has published numerous blogs and serves on multiple panels as an expert in the area of equity.

After years of working to dismantle oppressive structures in education, she was left with a lingering question....why would well-intentioned people continue to invest in systems that create barriers for children? What she realized is that when we step into our fullest potential we share, not abuse our power. Her first book, *Acts of Liberation*, is a journey of reflection and healing that is intended to help the reader find meaning in life's challenges. Additionally, this book provides a chance for readers to investigate different patterns in their life enabling them to explore how those patterns have led them to their present moment. Through her own exploration and insightful journey into her past, Dr. Green shows us that loving our broken pieces requires us to understand the inherent worth and value in all individuals. She strongly believes that when we harness our heart, it creates space to examine who we are and how we are showing up. It is her hope that this will ultimately assist the reader to find their soul purpose.

Made in the USA
Middletown, DE
06 September 2023